MARVELS OF TECHNOLOGY

ENERGY & HOME TECH

by
Anita Loughrey and Alex Woolf

Minneapolis, Minnesota

Credits

Cover and title page, © Andrew Jalbert/Adobe Stock and gong hangxu iStock; 4MR, © Byron Ortiz/Shutterstock; 4BR, © Blue Planet Studio/iStock; 4–5, © Iriana Shiyan/Adobe Stock and © Rido/Adobe Stock and © Alexey Boldin/Shutterstock; 6MR, © Designua/Shutterstock; 6BR, © Andrea Danti/Shutterstock; 6–7, © Smile Fight/Shutterstock; 7BL, © Public DomainWikimedia commons; 8MR, © tele52/Shutterstock; 8B, © Pepermpron/Shutterstock; 8–9, © marchello74/Shutterstock; 9TL, © Public Domain/Wellcome collection; 10BL, © Alejo Miranda/Shutterstock; 10–11, © Smileus/Shutterstock; 11TL, © Lex0077/Shutterstock; 11MR, © Jenson/Shutterstock; 11BL, © US Library of Congress/Wikimedia commons; 12B, © BlueRingMedia/Shutterstock; 12–13, © IndustryAndTravel/Shutterstock; 13T, © Designua/Shutterstock; 13BL, © Smithsonian Institution/Wikimedia commons; 14ML, © Kompass/Shutterstock; 14BR, © Photoongraphy/Shutterstock; 14–15, © Mark Borbely/Shutterstock; 15, © Macrovector/Shutterstock; 15BL, © SIMON Michou/Getty Images; 16TR, © DeiMosz/Shutterstock; 16M, © StockSmartStart/Shutterstock; 16BL, © Kair/Shutterstock; 16–17, © SeventyFour/Shutterstock; 17TR, © Siwakorn1933/Shutterstock; 18TR, © Martin Sanders/Beehive Illustration; 18ML, © Orange Deer studio/Shutterstock; 18B, © Designua/Shutterstock; 18–19, © Mark Sayer/Shutterstock; 19, © Artem Novosad/Shutterstock; 19BL, © Post of Romania/Wikimedia commons; 20MR, © BomMostFor/Shutterstock; 20BL, © Public domain/Wikimedia commons; 20–21, © Studio Light and Shade/Shutterstock; 21, © Martin Sanders/Beehive Illustration; 22TR, © the–lightwriter/iStock; 22ML, © Pixel–Shot/Shutterstock; 22BL, © Andrea Danti/Shutterstock; 22–23, © Pixel–Shot/Shutterstock; 23T, © Zhabska T.S./Shutterstock; 23BL, © Bettmann/Getty Images; 24M, © Martin Sanders/Beehive Illustration; 24BL, © Pangog200/Wikimedia commons; 24–25T, © pxl.store/Shutterstock; 24–25B, © VectorMine/Shutterstock; 25TR, © DSCimage/iStock; 26TR, © aphichart/iStock; 26BR, © Dmitry Kovalchuk/Shutterstock; 26–27, © Mooi Design/Shutterstock; 27TL, © Viacheslav Nikolaenko/Shutterstock; 28M, © Designua/Shutterstock; 28BL, © Public domain/Wikimedia commons; 28–29, © Chones/Shutterstock; 29TR, © Designua/Shutterstock; 29BR, © Designua/Shutterstock; 30ML, © Vadim Petrakov/Shutterstock; 30BL, © lloydcopeman.com/Wikimedia commons; 30–31, © Africa Studio/Shutterstock; 31TR, © Rainer Fuhrmann/Shutterstock; 32ML, © Designua/Shutterstock; 32–33T, © GiroScience/Shutterstock; 32–33B, © Designua/Shutterstock; 33TL, © Icon Craft Studio/Shutterstock; 33BL, © Andrey Starostin/Shutterstock; 34, © Martin Sanders/Beehive Illustration; 34–35, © 5 second Studio/Shutterstock; 35T, © Chadakorn Phalanon/Shutterstock; 35BL, © Olga_Bell/Shutterstock; 36, © DestinaDesign/Shutterstock; 36BL, © Public domain/Wikimedia commons; 36–37, © frantic00/Shutterstock; 37B, © VectorMine/Shutterstock; 38BR, © Martin Sanders/Beehive Illustration; 38–39, © PeopleImages.com –Yuri A/Shutterstock; 39TL, © Public domain/Wikimedia commons; 39MR, © Martin Sanders/Beehive Illustration; 40ML, © cunaplus/Shutterstock; 40BL, © Prostock–studio/Shutterstock; 40–41, © karamysh/Adobe Stock and sorapop/Adobe Stock; 41TL, © beeboys/Adobe Stock; 41T, © Nick Beer/Adobe Stock; 41TR, © AGPhotography/Adobe Stock; 41M, © bmak/Adobe Stock; 41BL, © ilbusca/iStock; 42ML, © BobNoah/Shutterstock; 42–43, © imaginima/iStock; 43ML, © onurdongel/iStock; 44BL, © BlueRingMedia/Shutterstock; 45TR, © Chones/Shutterstock; 45BL, © Blue Planet Studio/iStock; 47, © Jenson/Shutterstock

Bearport Publishing Company Product Development Team

President: Jen Jenson; Director of Product Development: Spencer Brinker; Managing Editor: Allison Juda; Associate Editor: Naomi Reich; Associate Editor: Tiana Tran; Art Director: Colin O'Dea; Designer: Kim Jones; Designer: Kayla Eggert; Product Development Assistant: Owen Hamlin

Statement on Usage of Generative Artificial Intelligence

Bearport Publishing remains committed to publishing high-quality nonfiction books. Therefore, we restrict the use of generative AI to ensure accuracy of all text and visual components pertaining to a book's subject. See BearportPublishing.com for details.

Library of Congress Cataloging-in-Publication Data is available at www.loc.gov or upon request from the publisher.

ISBN: 979-8-89232-084-9 (hardcover)
ISBN: 979-8-89232-616-2 (paperback)
ISBN: 979-8-89232-217-1 (ebook)

For more information, write to Bearport Publishing, 5357 Penn Avenue South, Minneapolis, MN 55419.

CONTENTS

Charging Our Lives

At its most basic, technology is simple. It's the application of scientific knowledge to create things that solve problems and make our lives easier, safer, and sometimes even more friendly to the environment. But what technology can do is pretty amazing.

Meeting Our Needs

New technologies are developed to meet the needs we have. For example, it's a lot of work to wash and dry clothes. But automatic washing machines can do most of that hard work for many people.

Solving Problems

Technology changes as our needs change. When fossil fuels are burned, they release carbon dioxide into the atmosphere, which traps heat. As a result, our planet is warming and our climate is changing. Solar power and biofuels are alternative energy sources that have been developed to reduce our use of fossil fuels and their associated heat-trapping gases being pumped into the atmosphere.

Designing the Home of Tomorrow

Every day, designers are working to solve global warming and climate change by developing ways to generate energy without burning fossil fuels. Their main goal is to make our energy sources cleaner and more sustainable while also making our homes safer and more comfortable.

Batteries

Batteries contain chemicals that store energy until needed. They provide a mobile source of power. Each battery has a positive and negative terminal. When the two terminals are connected by wires, they form a circuit. The circuit allows electrons to flow from the negative terminal to the positive terminal in order to power a device.

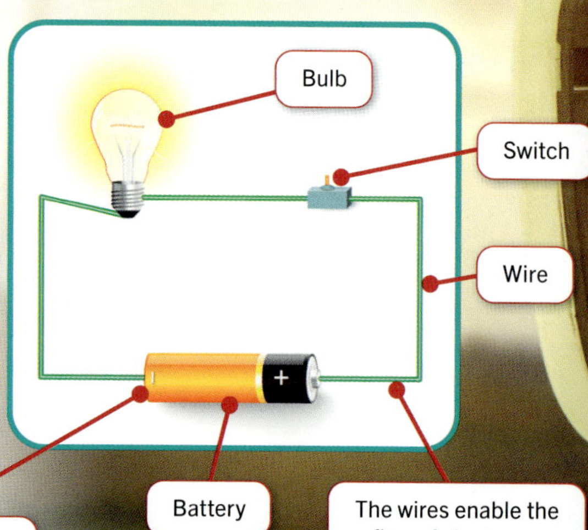

Rechargeable Batteries

Some batteries are rechargeable. A hybrid car engine turns a miniature electric generator, called an alternator, to feed electric current back into the battery to recharge it. The batteries in phones, tablets, and laptops use electricity from wall plugs to recharge. The electrical energy is converted into chemical energy inside the battery.

Positive terminal

Positive electrodes

Separators

Negative electrodes

When a battery is connected to an outside energy source, the electrons are forced out from the positive terminal and back to the negative terminal.

Negative terminal

DID YOU KNOW? Recycling your batteries is better for the environment.

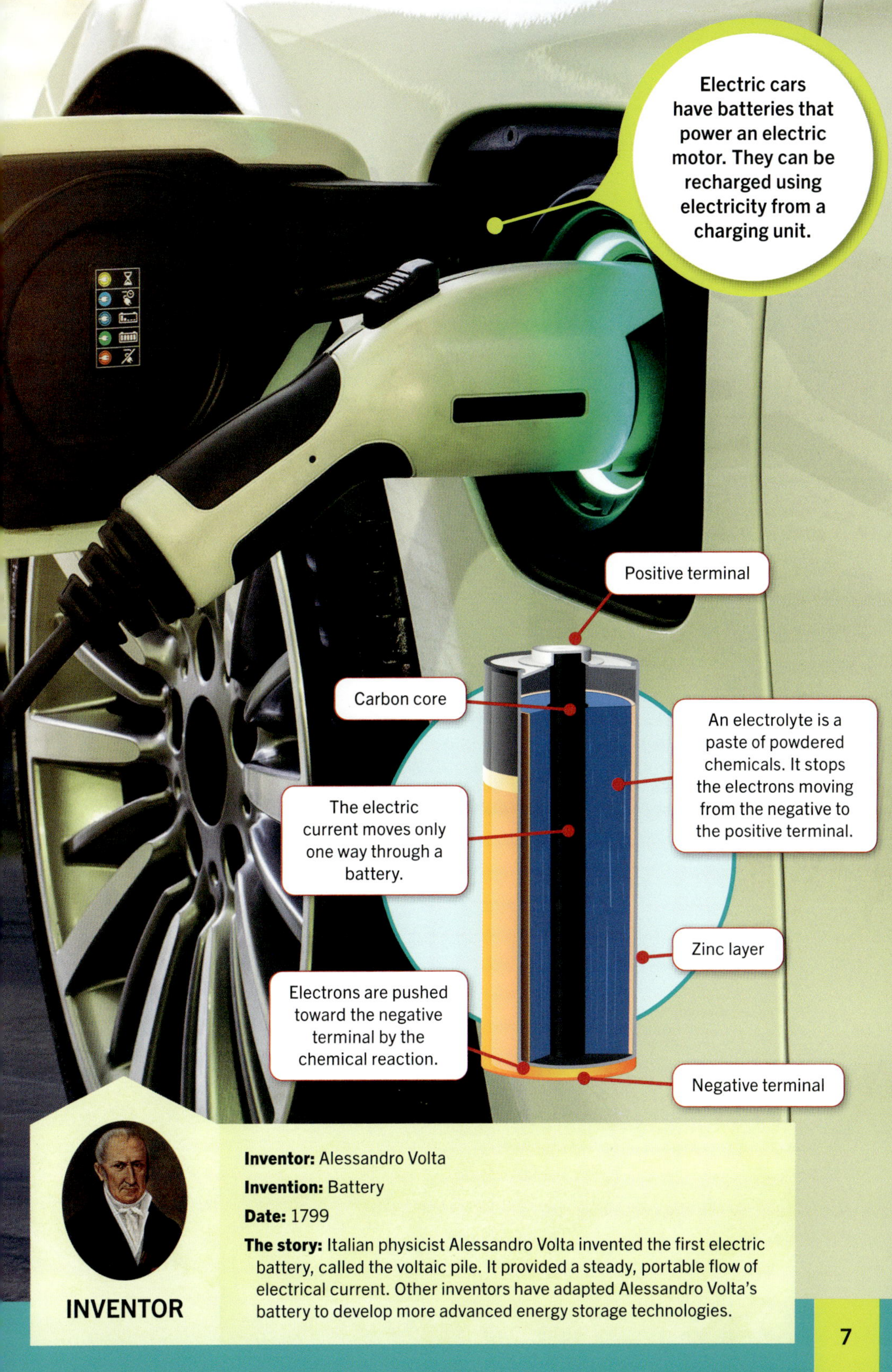

INVENTOR

Inventor: Alessandro Volta

Invention: Battery

Date: 1799

The story: Italian physicist Alessandro Volta invented the first electric battery, called the voltaic pile. It provided a steady, portable flow of electrical current. Other inventors have adapted Alessandro Volta's battery to develop more advanced energy storage technologies.

Electric Power

Electricity can be generated by burning fossil fuels, such as coal, oil, and gas. It can also be created by harnessing the power of wind, water, the sun, or nuclear reactions.

Hydropower

Dams store water in reservoirs. When water is released from the reservoir, the water flows through a turbine, making its blades rotate. The mechanical energy is converted into electrical energy, which creates power in the generator.

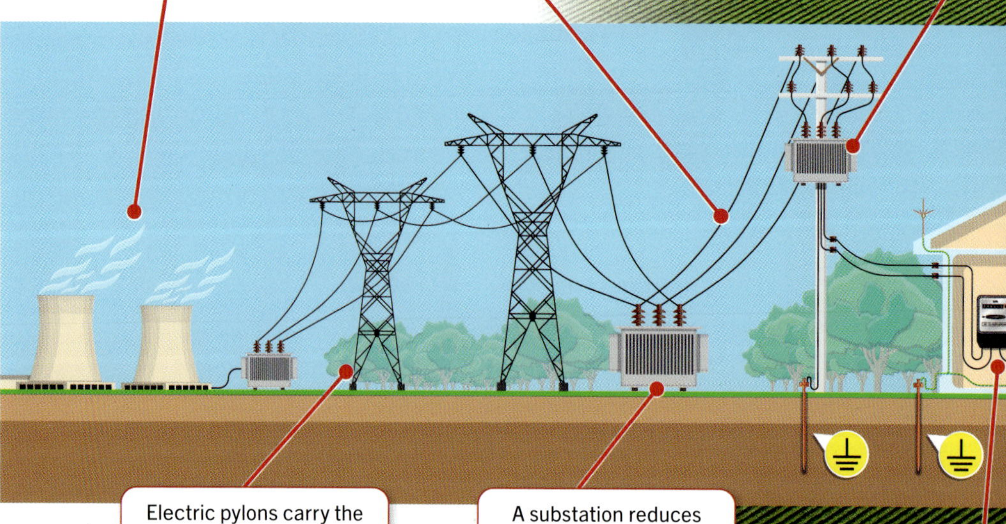

DID YOU KNOW? In 1882, Thomas Edison opened the first electric power plant. It sent power to 85 customers in New York City.

Solar Power

Solar cells convert sunlight into electricity and provide us with a clean, sustainable form of energy. Photons are particles of light. When photons hit a solar cell, they knock electrons free from their atoms. Metal contacts are attached to the positive and negative sides of the cell, forming an electrical circuit. The electrons flow through the circuit, which generates electricity.

Solar Cells

A solar cell is made from two layers of silicon sandwiched together. The top layer is treated with phosphorus and the bottom layer with boron. Phosphorus atoms have an extra electron that makes them negatively charged. Meanwhile, boron atoms are missing an electron and are positively charged. Photons from sunlight energize the electrons in the top layer, making them jump to the bottom layer. This creates an electrical current.

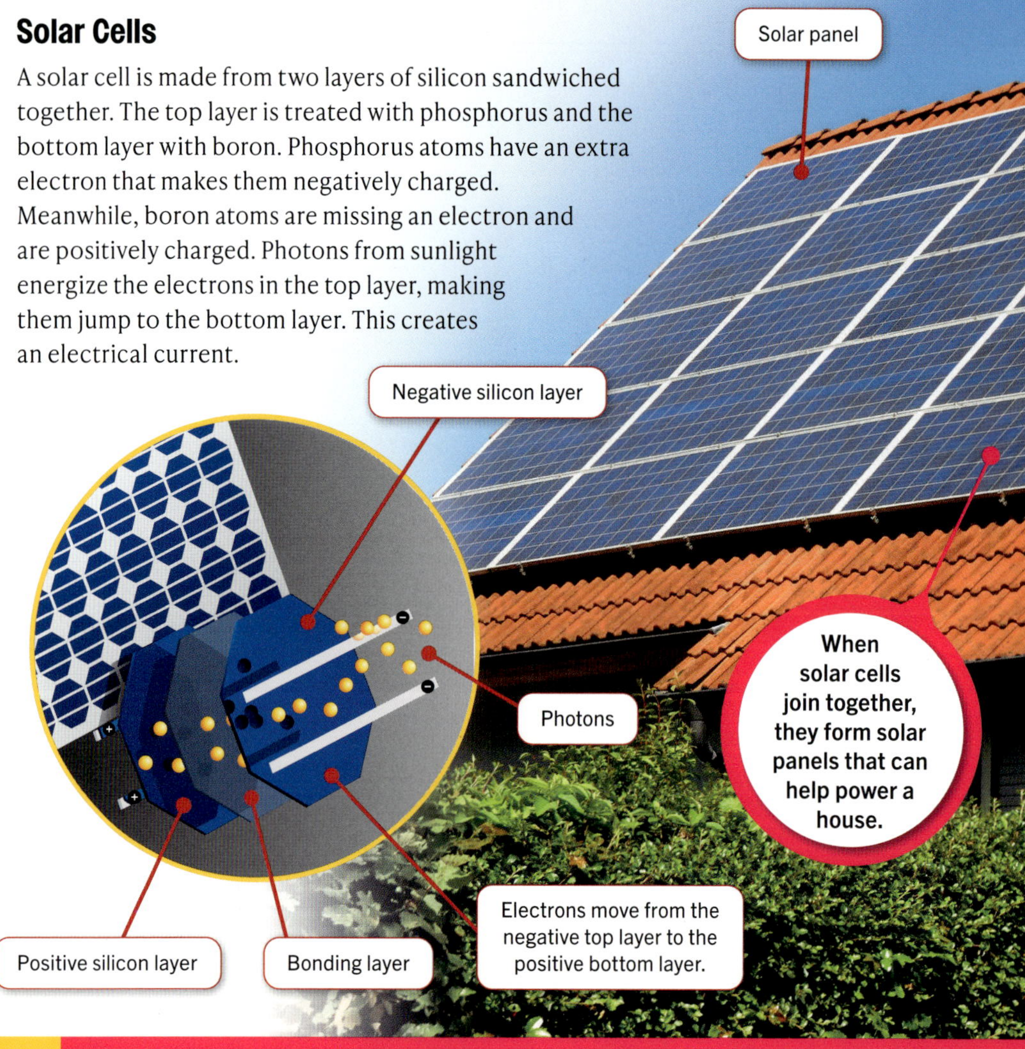

DID YOU KNOW? In 2016, Swiss pilot Bertrand Piccard was part of a team that flew a solar-powered plane around the world. The plane's only power source was the sun.

INVENTOR

Inventor: Mária Telkes

Invention: Solar heating

Date: 1948

The story: Hungarian-American scientist Mária Telkes invented a solar heating system that used large solar panels on the roof to collect sunlight. A special salt, called Glauber's salt, absorbed the heat and slowly released it into the house.

Nuclear Power

Nuclear power stations produce electricity by splitting uranium atoms in a process called nuclear fission. This process produces heat, which turns water to steam. The high-pressure steam turns a turbine that powers a generator to produce electricity. Highly radioactive nuclear waste is a by-product of nuclear fission. It must be disposed of safely—usually deep underground.

Safety Systems

Nuclear fission is a dangerous process that takes place in a nuclear reactor. In the reactor's core, fuel rods containing the uranium must be kept under cold water to prevent them from overheating. Control rods are inserted into the core to slow the chain reaction. If the core overheats, a coolant may be pumped in or the reactor is shut down. An overheating core can lead to an explosion, releasing harmful radiation into the environment.

Large cooling towers release the steam that powers the turbines.

This diagram shows how nuclear fission works.

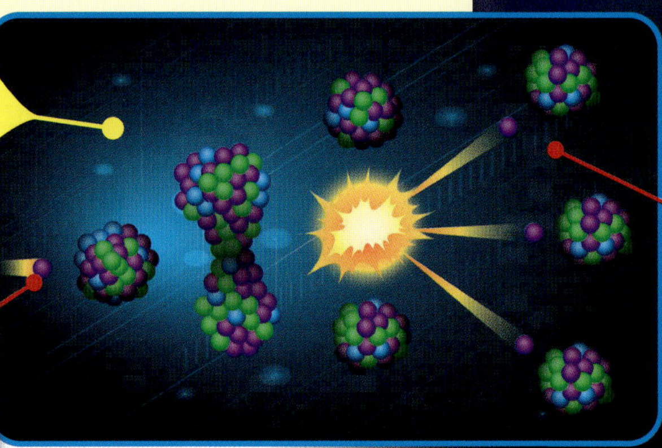

A neutron from a uranium atom hits the nucleus of another uranium atom, causing it to split.

As more neutrons are created, more neutrons strike other uranium nuclei. This causes a chain reaction.

DID YOU KNOW? The sun is a large nuclear reactor. It uses a natural process of fusion to produce energy in the form of heat and light.

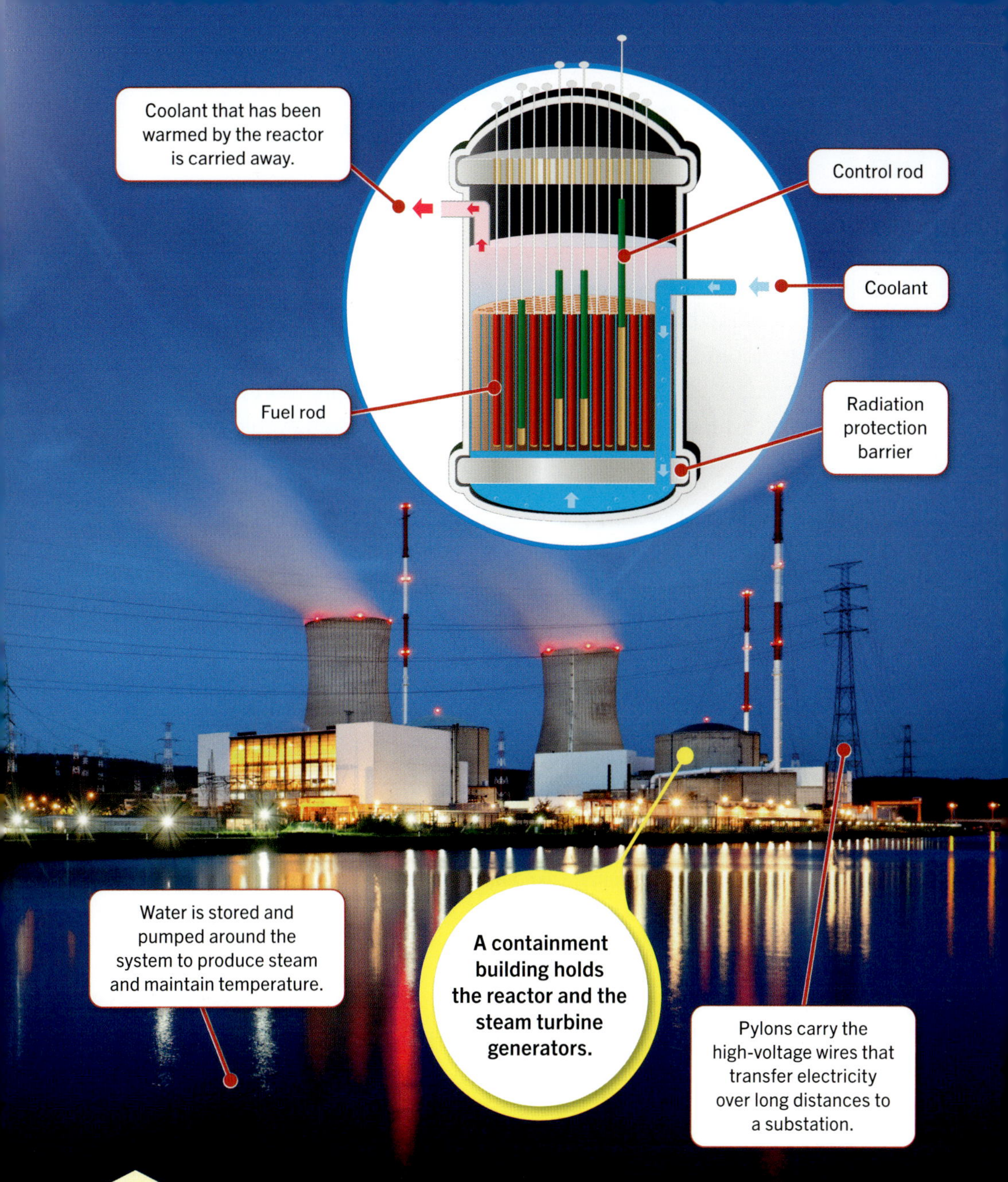

Coolant that has been warmed by the reactor is carried away.

Control rod

Coolant

Fuel rod

Radiation protection barrier

Water is stored and pumped around the system to produce steam and maintain temperature.

A containment building holds the reactor and the steam turbine generators.

Pylons carry the high-voltage wires that transfer electricity over long distances to a substation.

INVENTOR

Inventor: Lise Meitner

Discovery: Nuclear fission

Date: 1939

The story: Austrian-Swedish physicist Lise Meitner helped discover that uranium atoms stretch out when bombarded by neutrons. She also found that some of the uranium atoms split apart into two smaller, much lighter atoms called barium and krypton. Together, these atoms may convert mass into energy.

Bioenergy

When plants and animals die, their organic matter begins to decompose, or rot. As this material breaks down, it releases gas. The energy contained in the gas can be harnessed in different ways to create liquid fuel, electricity, and heat. This is known as bioenergy. It is derived from the decomposing organic matter all around us, which makes bioenergy both plentiful and renewable.

There are three ways to capture and harness the energy contained within organic matter. The matter can be burned, changed to a liquid or gas fuel, or decomposed by microorganisms. Burning wood to generate heat is the most common example of bioenergy at work. Fuels created from organic matter can be used in vehicles, in power plants, and to heat and light homes.

Ethanol is a biofuel most commonly made from corn. When added to gasoline, it helps reduce harmful emissions from vehicles.

First-generation biofuels are made from food crops, such as sugarcane and corn. The sugars in these crops are broken down by microorganisms to create a fuel that can be added to gasoline or placed within a fuel cell that generates electricity. Second-generation biofuels are made from non-food organic matter, such as the unused stems, leaves, and husks of food crops. These materials can also be burned or broken down to create various gas fuels.

DID YOU KNOW? When burned, biofuels release less heat-trapping carbon dioxide into the atmosphere than fossil fuels.

Water waste

Organic matter

Animal waste

Food waste

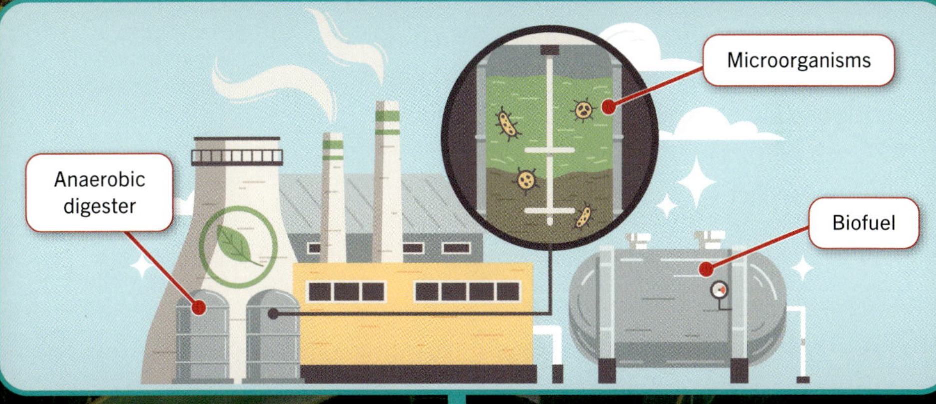

Bio-oil

Gas

Warmth

Electricity

INVENTOR

Inventor: Jean Pain

The invention: Compost heater

Date: 1970s

The story: Jean Pain inserted tubes into tall piles of rotting organic materials, or compost, to extract heat and gas. He managed to get all the heat, hot water, and electricity his home and farm needed using his compost pile.

Recycling Facilities

Materials for recycling are brought to a recycling plant in large trucks. Sometimes, the materials have been pre-sorted, and other times they are sorted at the recycling plant. The trucks empty the recyclable material onto conveyor belts. Any pieces of paper and cardboard are separated to be sent to paper mills. A separator pushes plastic and metal containers another way.

Materials that can be recycled have the international recycling symbol on them.

Magnetic Sorters

Metal cans can be sorted using magnets. A rotating magnet above the conveyor belt grabs steel metal cans and pulls them away. Under the conveyor belt, there may be a magnetized rotor that repels non-iron-containing metal cans and causes the cans to jump off the belt and into another collection bin.

Different materials are recycled in different ways.

INVENTION

Inventor: Azza Abdel Hamid Faiad

Invention: A catalyst to produce biofuel

Date: 2012

The story: Egyptian Azza Abdel Hamid Faiad discovered a way to recycle plastic waste by using a catalyst called aluminosilicate. The catalyst breaks down plastic waste to produce gases such as methane, which can be converted into the biofuel ethanol.

DID YOU KNOW? It can take less than a week to turn old newspapers, books, and magazines into new ones.

Running Water

Would you believe the running water in our homes may start as rain? The rain falls from the sky and filters into the earth to become groundwater. Water companies pump this water into a water treatment plant, where any waste matter is removed, and the water is cleaned and treated. During dry spells, when there isn't enough groundwater, water is taken from reservoirs. This water is pumped through a network of pipes and into our homes.

An infrared sensor can detect a user's hands and sends out a signal to start water at a sink.

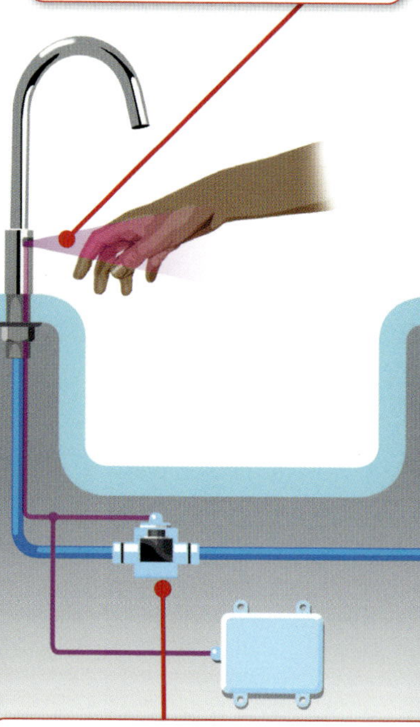

The signal is sent to a solenoid valve, a device that turns an electrical signal into motion. The valve starts the water flow.

When a toilet is flushed, a valve opens in the tank, letting water flow into the bowl.

When a tap is turned, the screw in a pipe rises, which lifts a washer. This lets the water flow.

When the handle is turned the other way, the washer is screwed down. This stops the flow of water.

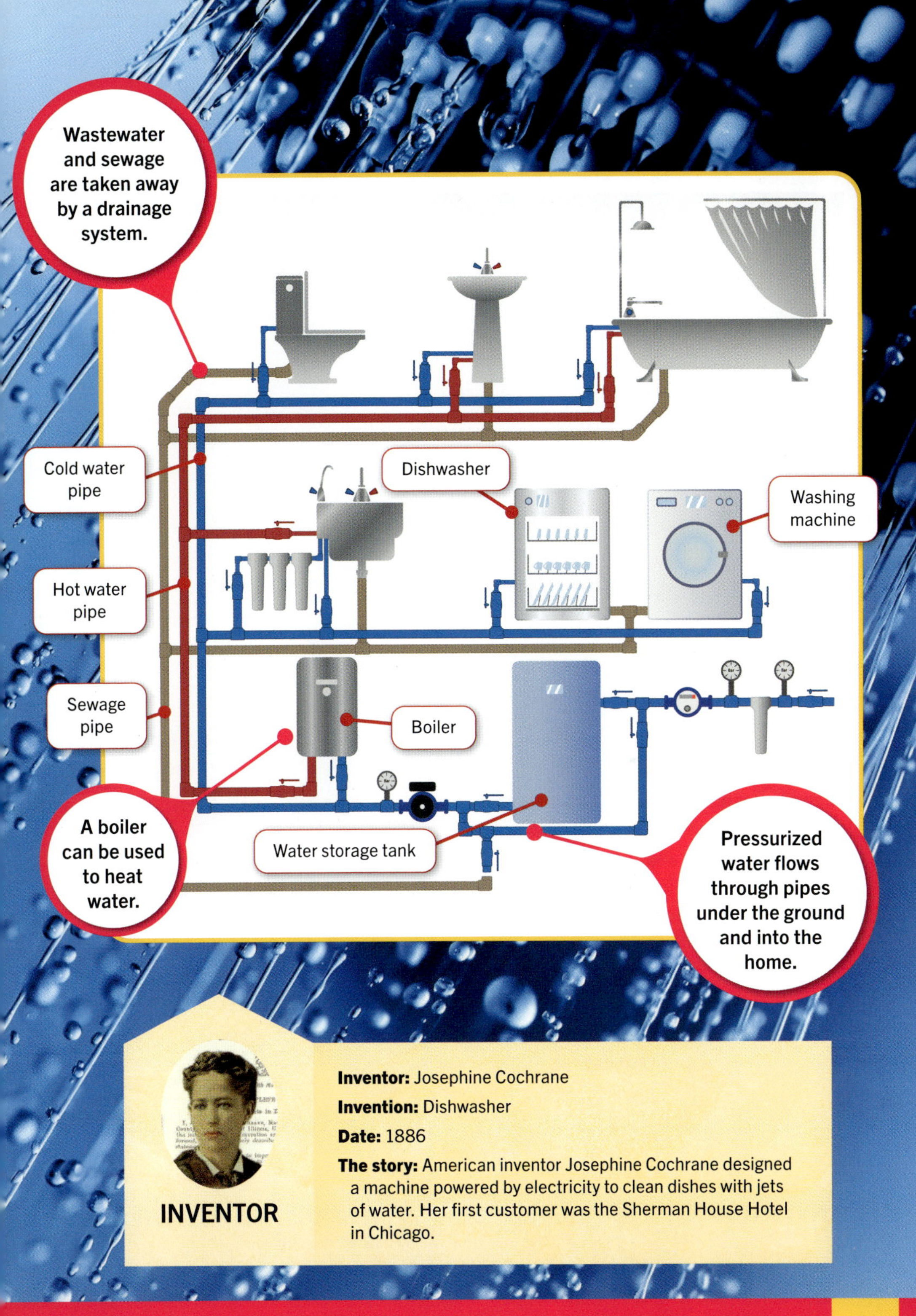

INVENTOR

Inventor: Josephine Cochrane

Invention: Dishwasher

Date: 1886

The story: American inventor Josephine Cochrane designed a machine powered by electricity to clean dishes with jets of water. Her first customer was the Sherman House Hotel in Chicago.

DID YOU KNOW? Keeping the water running while brushing your teeth can waste almost 4 gallons (15 L) of water.

Washing Machines

Washing machines contain two drums. The inner, rotating drum holds the clothes. Meanwhile, the outer one holds the water, which flows into and out of the inner drum during the washing process. A heating element can warm up the water, and a thermostat checks its temperature. An electric pump removes the water from the drum. When the wash cycle is finishing, one pipe sends clean water into the machine, and another pipe lets out the wastewater.

The Programmer

An electronic device, called a programmer, makes a washing machine go through a series of steps. First, the machine washes and rinses the clothes. Then, it spins them to remove water.

With a top-loading washing machine, clothes are loaded through a door at the top.

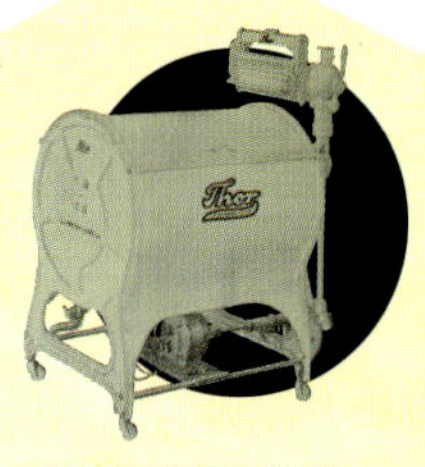

INVENTION

Inventor: Alva J. Fisher

Invention: Electric washing machine

Date: 1901

The story: American engineer Alva J. Fisher invented the first electric washing machine. The machine consisted of a rotating cylinder filled with several spikes to hold down the clothes. It made eight rotations clockwise, then changed direction. As the machine did not have an on or off switch, the only way to stop the machine was by pulling the plug out.

DID YOU KNOW? In 1916, powder laundry detergent was invented for washing machine use. This detergent helps remove stains from clothes.

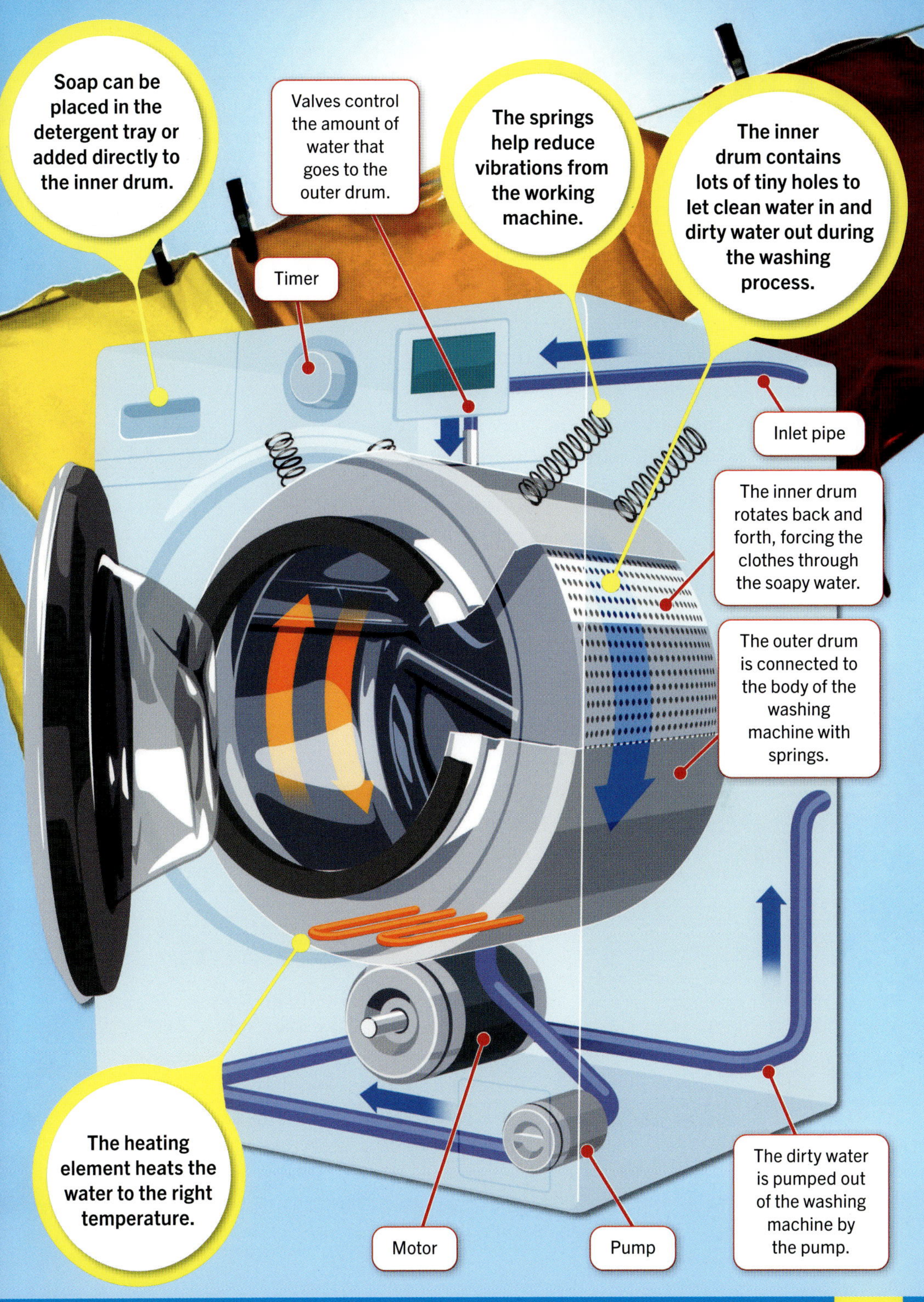
Soap can be placed in the detergent tray or added directly to the inner drum.
Valves control the amount of water that goes to the outer drum.
The springs help reduce vibrations from the working machine.
The inner drum contains lots of tiny holes to let clean water in and dirty water out during the washing process.
Timer
Inlet pipe
The inner drum rotates back and forth, forcing the clothes through the soapy water.
The outer drum is connected to the body of the washing machine with springs.
The heating element heats the water to the right temperature.
Motor
Pump
The dirty water is pumped out of the washing machine by the pump.

Toilets

One of the modern conveniences we should be most thankful for is the flush toilet. Before its invention, people used outhouses, which were holes dug into the ground, often covered by a small shelter. The raw sewage from an outhouse went into nearby lakes, rivers, and oceans. If people did not want to leave their warm homes to use outhouses in the cold outdoors, they had relieve themselves in pots and pans that were then emptied outside.

A modern flush toilet is a ceramic bowl connected to a drain. After a person uses it, they press a button or push down on a handle that releases water stored in a tank above and behind the bowl. This water pours into the bowl and is directed into a swirling flow that takes the waste down.

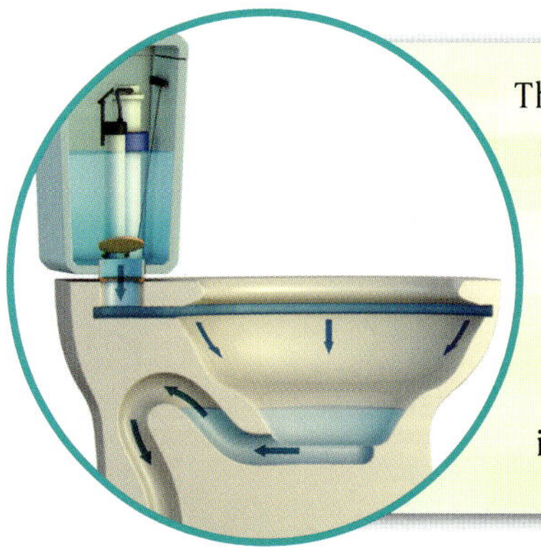

The water's swirling motion helps rinse and clean the bowl of any solid and liquid waste that clings to it. The wastewater empties from the bowl and is carried by pipes to either a sewer or a septic tank. At the same time, the tank refills with water and is ready for the next flush.

DID YOU KNOW? A plumber named Sir Thomas Crapper thought of ways to improve the flush toilet. He added the U-bend pipe that traps toilet and sewer gases.

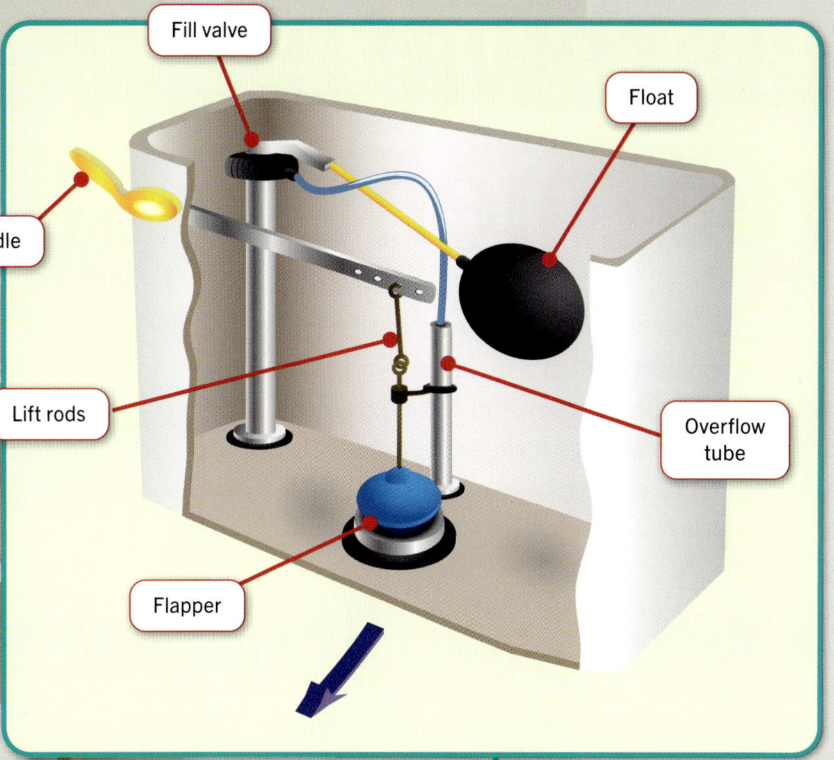

Fill valve

Float

Handle

Lift rods

Overflow tube

Flapper

Before the invention of toilet paper, people used sticks, moss, leaves, and other natural materials to wipe and clean themselves.

INVENTOR

Inventor: Sir John Harington

The invention: The Ajax flush toilet

Date: 1596

The story: John Harington designed England's first flush toilet, featuring a water tank that released water into the bowl to empty and clean it. He installed an Ajax toilet for his godmother, Queen Elizabeth I.

Wastewater Treatment

Wastewater, or sewage, must be treated so that it does not harm the environment. There are two types of wastewater treatment: primary and secondary. The primary treatment starts with the wastewater flowing through a screen to remove large objects. It is soon moved into a grit chamber, where sand and small stones settle to the bottom. Then, the wastewater passes through a sedimentation tank. The tank is where suspended organic matter settles to the bottom to form sludge. This sludge can be dried and sold to farmers as fertilizer or burned to generate electricity.

In some plants, wastewater is passed through a trickling filter system as a secondary treatment.

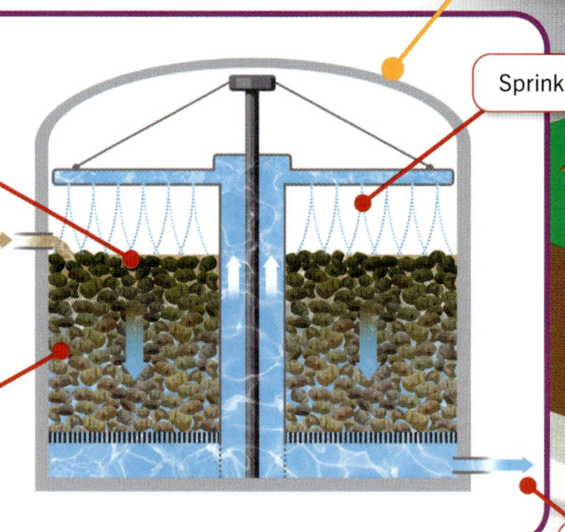

INVENTOR

Inventor: Deepika Kurup

Invention: Solar-powered water purification system

Date: 2012

The story: American Deepika Kurup invented a way to purify water at the age of 14. She was inspired by seeing children in India drinking dirty water. Deepika Kurup combined titanium dioxide with cement. It cleans water by speeding up the sun's disinfection process.

Secondary Treatment

After leaving the sedimentation tank, the wastewater is pumped into an aeration tank. This tank is where the wastewater is mixed with air and an activated, or bacteria-filled, sludge. The bacteria in the sludge breaks down the organic matter remaining in the wastewater and converts it into harmless by-products. Then, the purified liquid waste is discharged into rivers and streams.

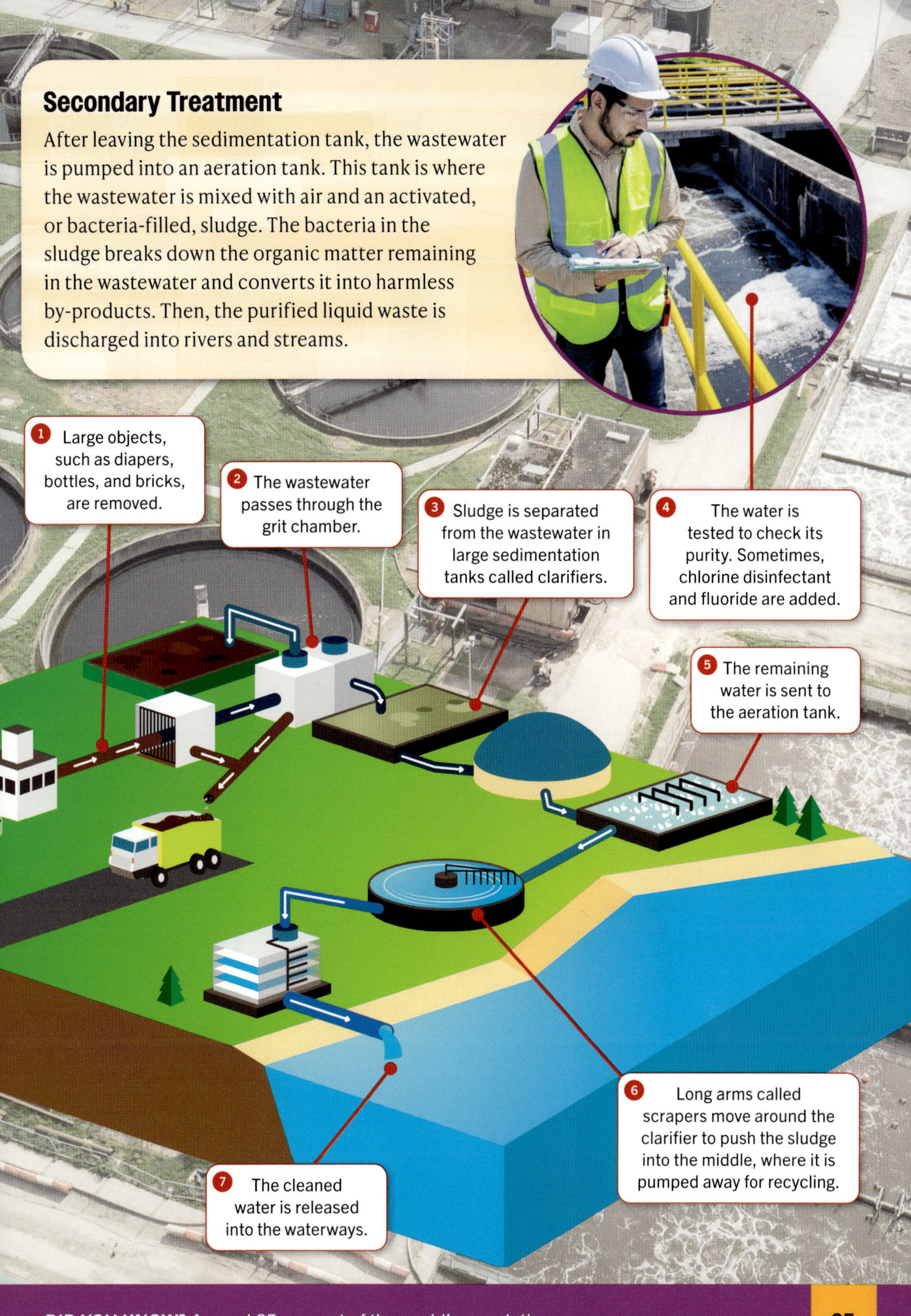

DID YOU KNOW? Around 25 percent of the world's population does not have access to clean drinking water.

Gray Water

In most older homes, all the used water ends up in a wastewater treatment plant. It flows through the house's plumbing system, into a sewer or septic tank, and is transported to the plant to be treated and reused. Some newer homes, however, are designed to hold on to some of their untreated wastewater and find uses for it around the house, yard, and garden.

Any used household water that has not come into contact with feces, or poop, is called gray water. It is the water that flows out of bathroom sinks, showers, tubs, dishwashers, and washing machines. There are several kinds of gray water systems a home can use, but most of them start by diverting used water from the main sewage pipes. The system then filters out some floating debris and contaminants and collects the water in a storage tank, where it is pumped outdoors through irrigation tubes.

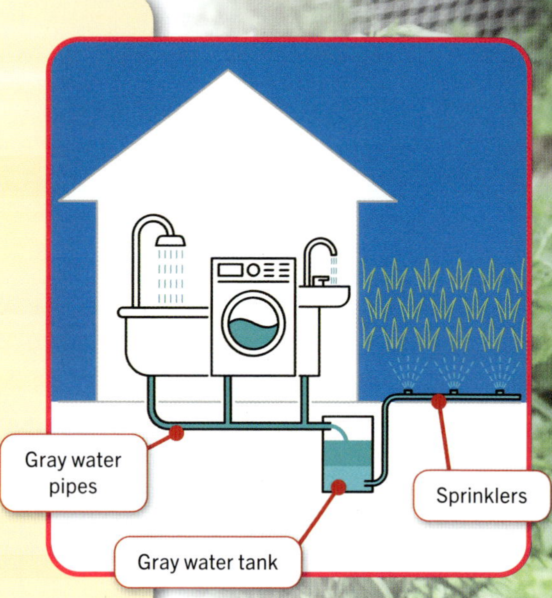

DID YOU KNOW? Using gray water to flush toilets and irrigate plants can save a household as much as 15,000 gal. (56,781 L) of water per year!

One simple way to collect and use gray water is to gather cold water in a bucket as you wait for your bath or shower water to heat up. Instead of flushing, you can pour gray water into toilets to flush them, saving a lot of water. About 65 percent of a household's total wastewater is produced by toilet flushing.

It's best to use stored gray water within 24 hours of it being gathered. This prevents bacteria from growing, which may cause a bad smell.

INVENTION

Inventor: Mehaa Amirthalingam

The invention: The Arya gray water filtering device

The story: During a severe drought in Cape Town, South Africa, 14-year-old Mehaa Amirthalingam invented a device that blocks the flow of fresh water into a toilet during flushing. Her invention used only gray water to rinse and empty the toilet bowl. This device can save as much as 25 gal. (95 L) of fresh drinking water per person per day.

Light Bulbs

An incandescent light bulb has a simple structure. At the base are two metal contacts, which are the ends of an electrical circuit. These pieces of metal are attached to a very thin filament made of a metallic element called tungsten. The filament is housed within a glass bulb filled with an inert, or non-reactive, gas, such as argon.

Tungsten is used as a filament because it has an extremely high melting point.

Incandescent Bulbs

When the incandescent light bulb is attached to a power supply, an electric current flows from one contact to the other, passing through the wires and filament. Since tungsten is resistant to the flow of electricity, it quickly heats up and releases energy in the form of light. The filament gets extremely hot, but it doesn't burn because there is only inert gas inside the glass bulb.

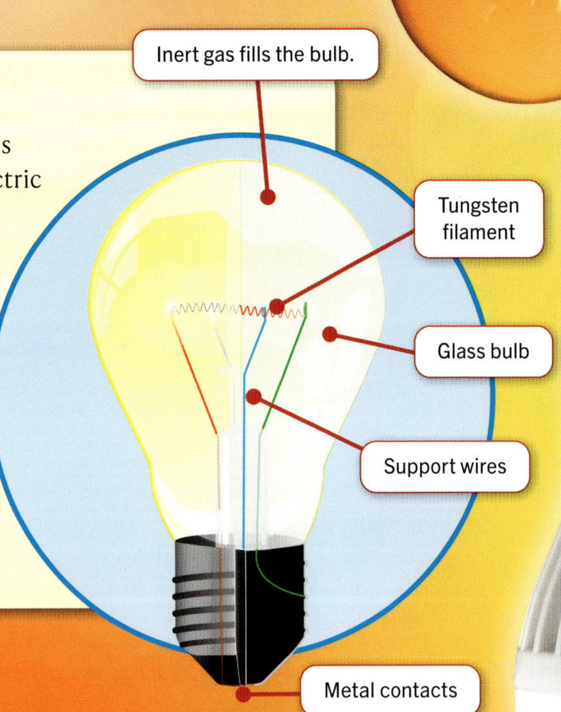

INVENTOR

Inventor: Nick Holonyak Jr.

Invention: LED bulb

Date: 1962

The story: American engineer Nick Holonyak Jr. invented the first practical light-emitting diode (LED) device. LEDs don't have a filament that will burn out or get very hot. The movement of electrons in a semiconductor material causes the light in these bulbs.

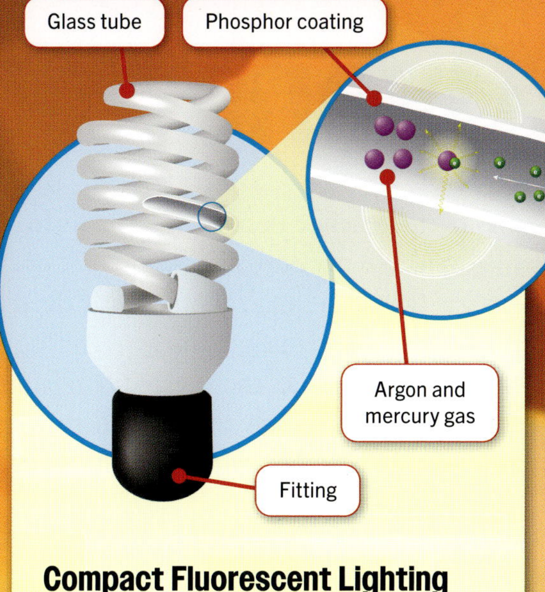

Compact Fluorescent Lighting

A compact fluorescent light (CFL) is a type of light bulb. Inside it, an electric current interacts with argon and mercury gas to create ultraviolet light. The phosphor coating converts this into visible light.

Solid-State Lighting

Solid-state lighting (SSL) uses LEDs as a source of illumination. SSL lights are energy-efficient and durable. They are used in traffic lights, flashlights, searchlights, and headlights.

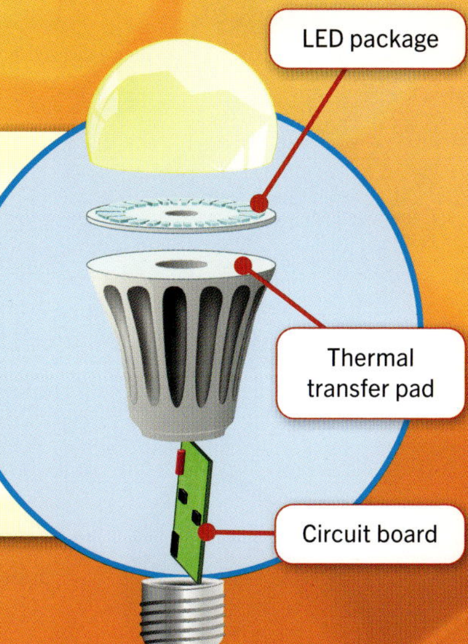

DID YOU KNOW? An incandescent light bulb converts 10 percent of its energy into light. In an LED, nearly 100 percent of the energy becomes light.

Ovens

Gas ovens generate heat using a gas-fueled burner. When the oven's temperature dial is raised, it opens a valve. This lets gas flow to a small, continuously burning flame called a pilot light. The flame gets bigger, igniting the burner. When the oven has reached the selected temperature, a thermostat shuts off the gas supply to the burner, switching it on again only when the temperature starts to drop.

Electric Ovens

Electric ovens contain top and bottom heating elements. These elements are heated by electrical power, which heats the cooking compartment. When the right temperature is reached, the thermostat sends a signal to the circuit board to cut the power to the elements. Convection ovens have a fan to blow the hot air around the oven.

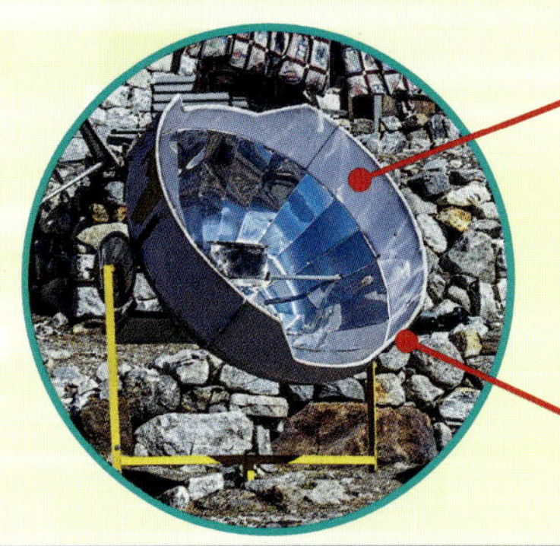

Solar ovens cook using the sun's rays. The rays are all reflected to a central place in the oven, so the heat energy from all the rays adds up to make it very hot.

Silver surfaces reflect the heat of the sun into the cooking compartment.

INVENTOR

Inventor: Lloyd Groff Copeman

Invention: Electric oven

Date: 1912

The story: American inventor Lloyd Groff Copeman designed the first electric oven. It was made from a wooden frame housing two metal boxes. His design included a thermostat to control the heating element and an automatic timer to turn the oven on or off at a set time.

Induction Cooktops

An induction cooktop consists of a ceramic surface with an electromagnetic coil beneath it. When the cooktop is switched on, an electric current passes through the coil, creating a magnetic field. This induces several small electric currents in the base of a saucepan or pot placed on the cooktop. The heat comes from the pans or pots themselves. Induction cooking is highly efficient and provides consistent heat and excellent temperature control. However, only stainless steel or iron pots and pans can be used.

DID YOU KNOW? An oven used in the metal industry is called a furnace. One used for making pottery is called a kiln.

Microwave Ovens

Microwave ovens cook food using high-powered electromagnetic waves, known as microwaves. A device called a magnetron converts electricity from the electrical outlet into microwaves. It sends electricity into the oven through a tube called a waveguide. The microwaves penetrate the food, making the molecules inside it vibrate, which makes the food heat up.

Microwaves have wavelengths greater than those of visible light.

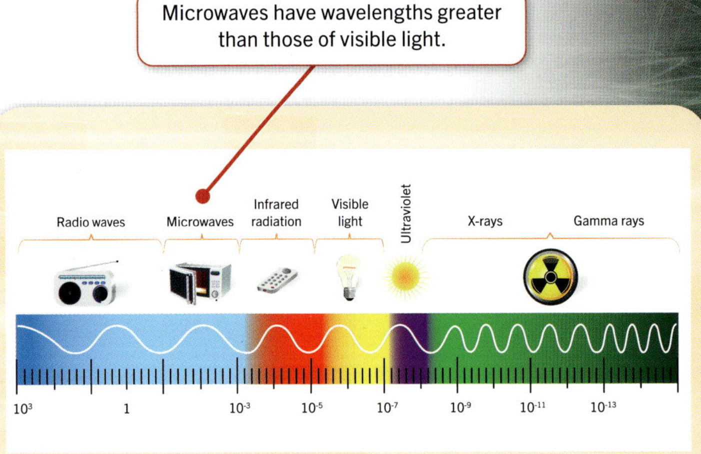

Electromagnetic Spectrum

The electromagnetic spectrum is made up of different types of energy, each with their own wavelength. Microwaves are very high energy but can harm living tissue. This is why microwave ovens have thick metal walls.

The door contains a metal mesh with small holes. This can stop microwaves from escaping while letting visible light out, so we can see into the cooking compartment.

DID YOU KNOW? It is possible to transmit data using microwaves. They are used by NASA for deep space communication.

INVENTION

Inventor: Percy Spencer

Invention: Microwave oven

Date: 1947

The story: American engineer Percy Spencer was experimenting with microwaves when a magnetron melted candy in his pocket. He tried placing popcorn kernels near the magnetron, and they popped. This discovery led him to design the microwave oven.

Microwaves bounce off the reflective walls of the cooking compartment and into the food.

The waveguide directs the microwaves into the cooking compartment.

Cooling fan

The magnetron contains two spinning ring magnets that heat electrons from the electricity and generate the microwaves.

The capacitor boosts the power supply to the magnetron.

Microwaves heat the moisture inside the popcorn kernels, which makes them pop.

The turntable rotates so the food cooks evenly.

The transformer reduces the voltage of the electricity from the electrical source so the microwave can operate.

Refrigerators

The technology of refrigerators is based on a simple principle. When a gas is compressed, it gets warmer. If the gas expands, it cools. A pipe that runs partly inside and outside the refrigerator is filled with gas. The gas is compressed outside the refrigerator, while inside the refrigerator the pipe widens, expanding and cooling the gas to a liquid.

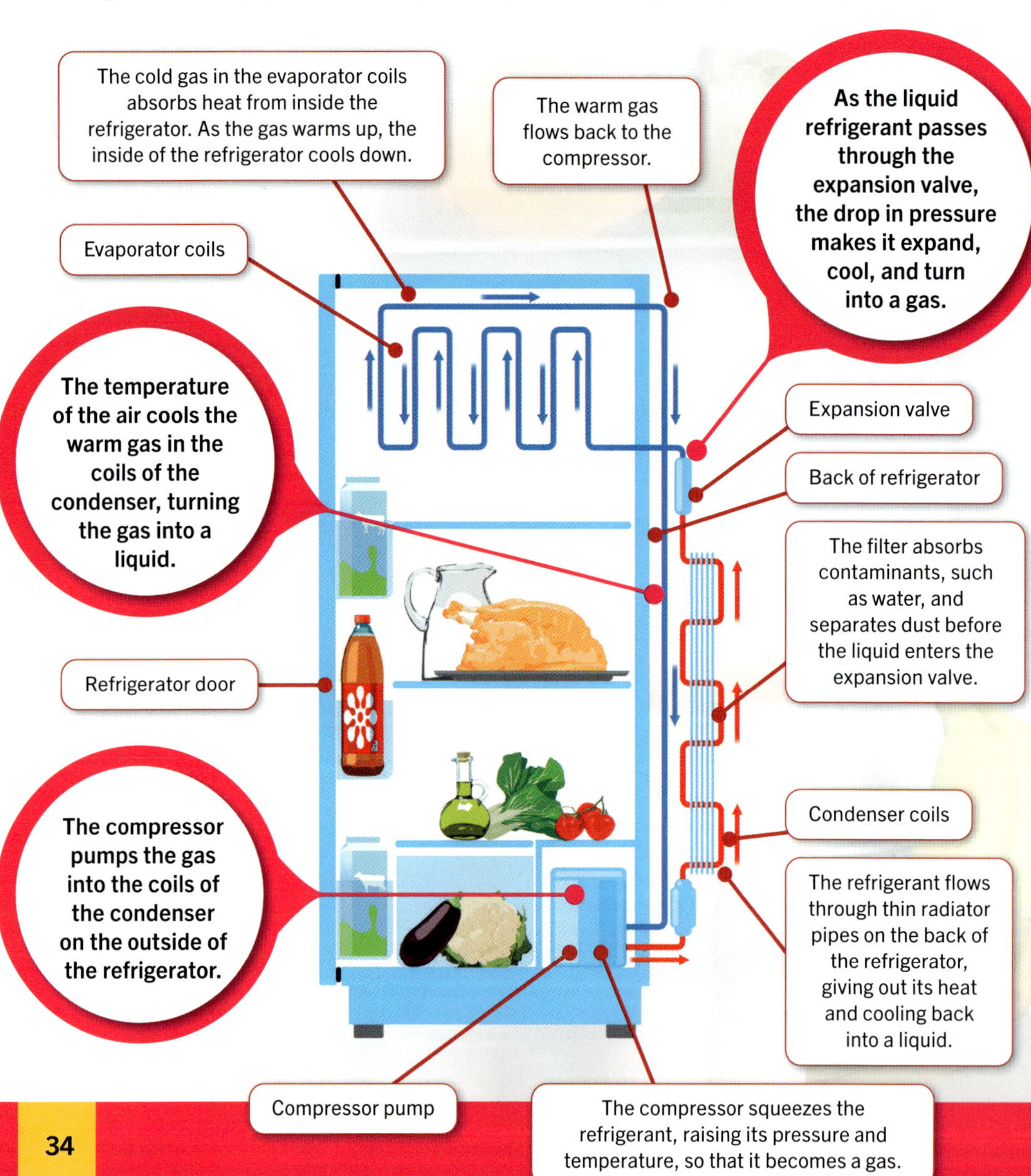

The thermostat controls the temperature of the refrigerator by switching the compressor on and off.

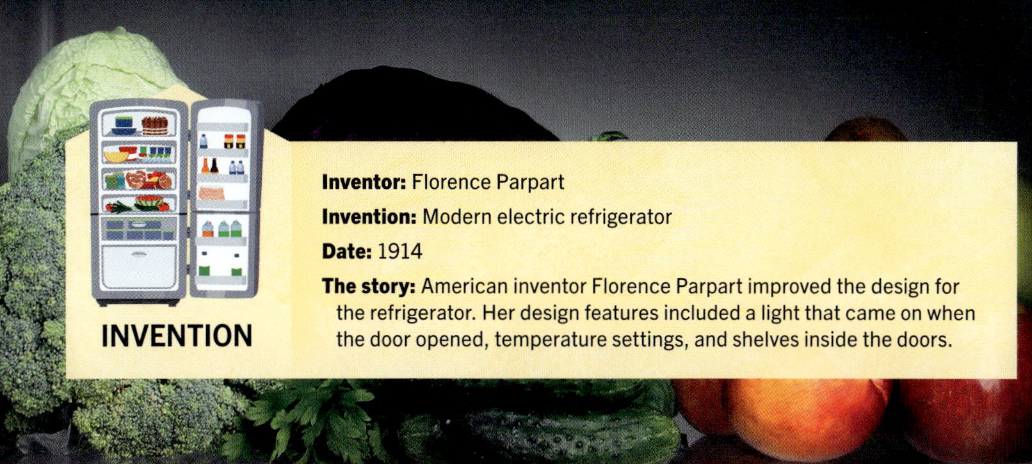

INVENTION

Inventor: Florence Parpart

Invention: Modern electric refrigerator

Date: 1914

The story: American inventor Florence Parpart improved the design for the refrigerator. Her design features included a light that came on when the door opened, temperature settings, and shelves inside the doors.

DID YOU KNOW? One of the world's largest refrigeration units keeps the Large Hadron Collider particle accelerator at CERN, a physics laboratory, cool.

Thermoses

Thermoses keep cold liquids cold and hot liquids hot by preventing the flow of heat. Heat always flows from a warmer place to a cooler place. It can be transferred by conduction, convection, and radiation. A thermos prevents heat from transferring.

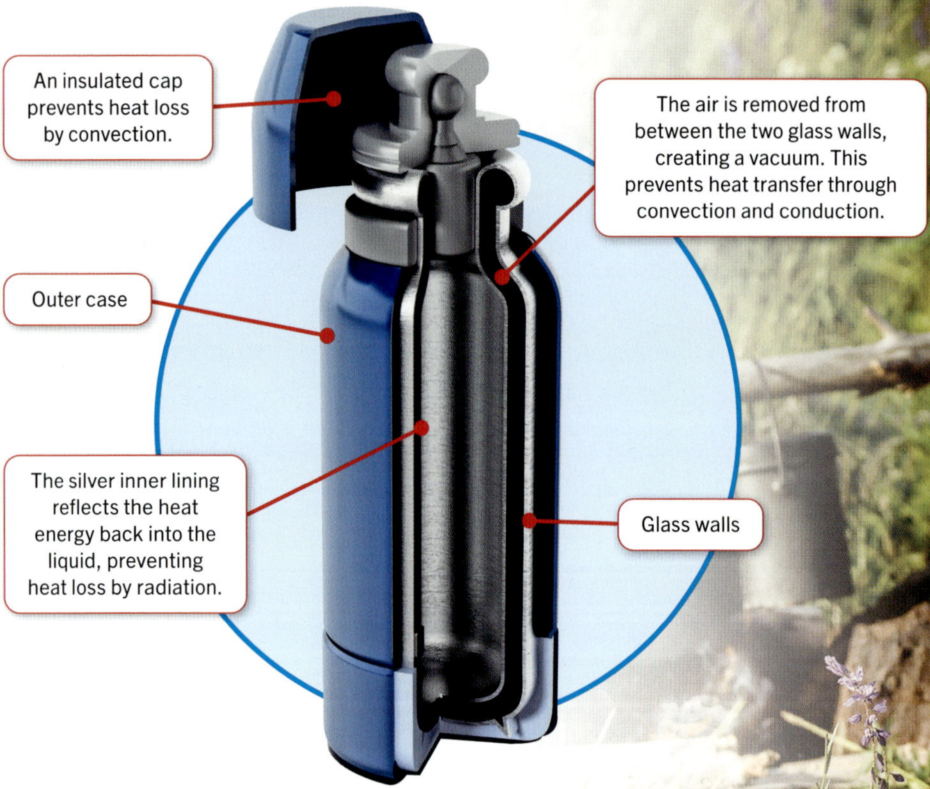

An insulated cap prevents heat loss by convection.

The air is removed from between the two glass walls, creating a vacuum. This prevents heat transfer through convection and conduction.

Outer case

The silver inner lining reflects the heat energy back into the liquid, preventing heat loss by radiation.

Glass walls

INVENTOR

Inventor: James Dewar

Invention: Thermos

Date: 1892

The story: Scottish chemist and physicist Sir James Dewar invented the Dewar flask, which later became known as the thermos, to study how gas can be changed into a liquid. His aim was to keep the liquefied gas as cold as possible.

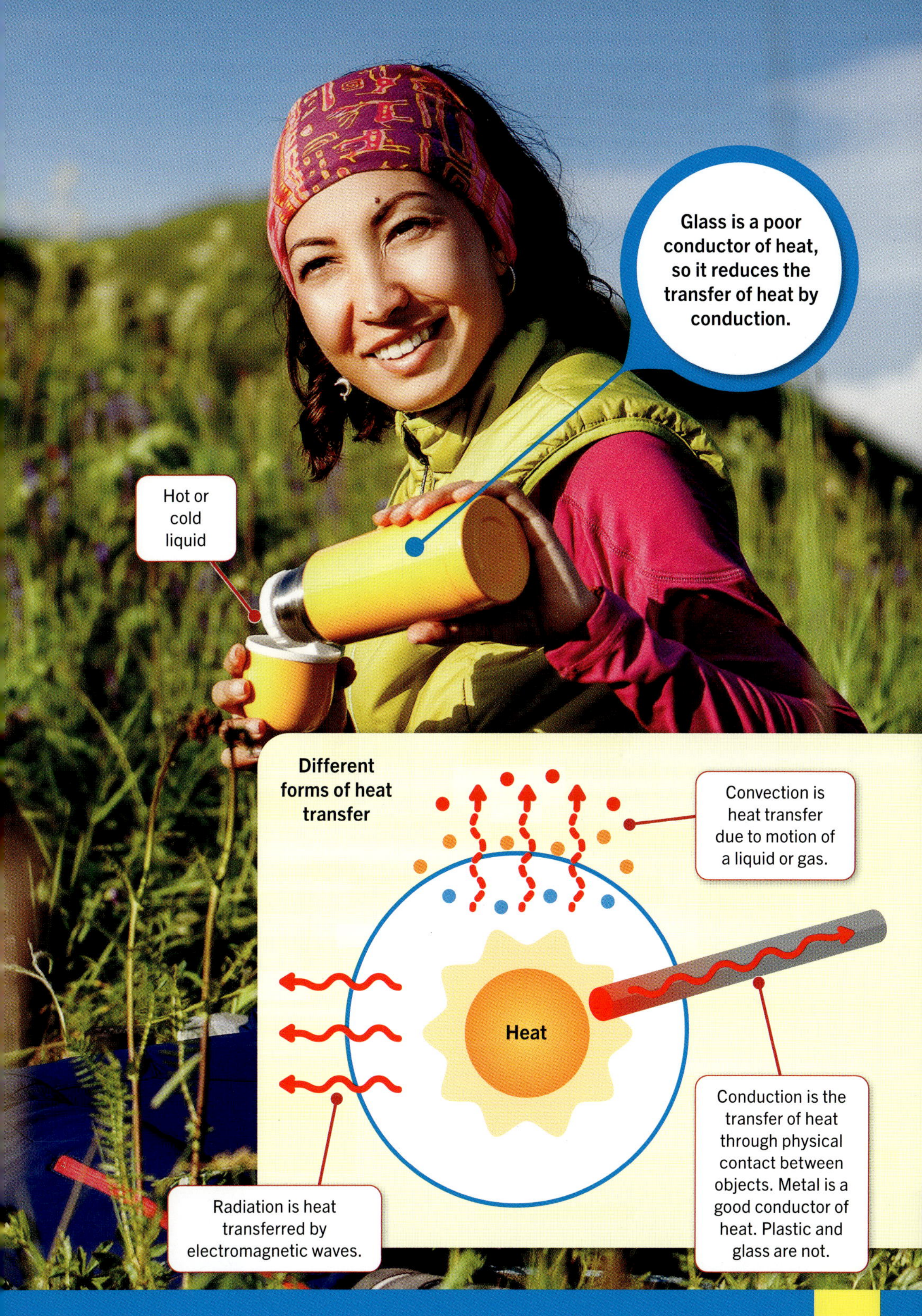

DID YOU KNOW? The liquid fuel used in space rockets is kept cold using thermos technology.

Hair Dryers

A hair dryer has a long, thin coil of wire inside of it. This wire acts as a heating element, which converts electrical energy into heat energy. A motor drives a fan that draws air in through holes in the side of the hair dryer. The air is warmed as it passes over the heating element before being blown out of the front of the dryer.

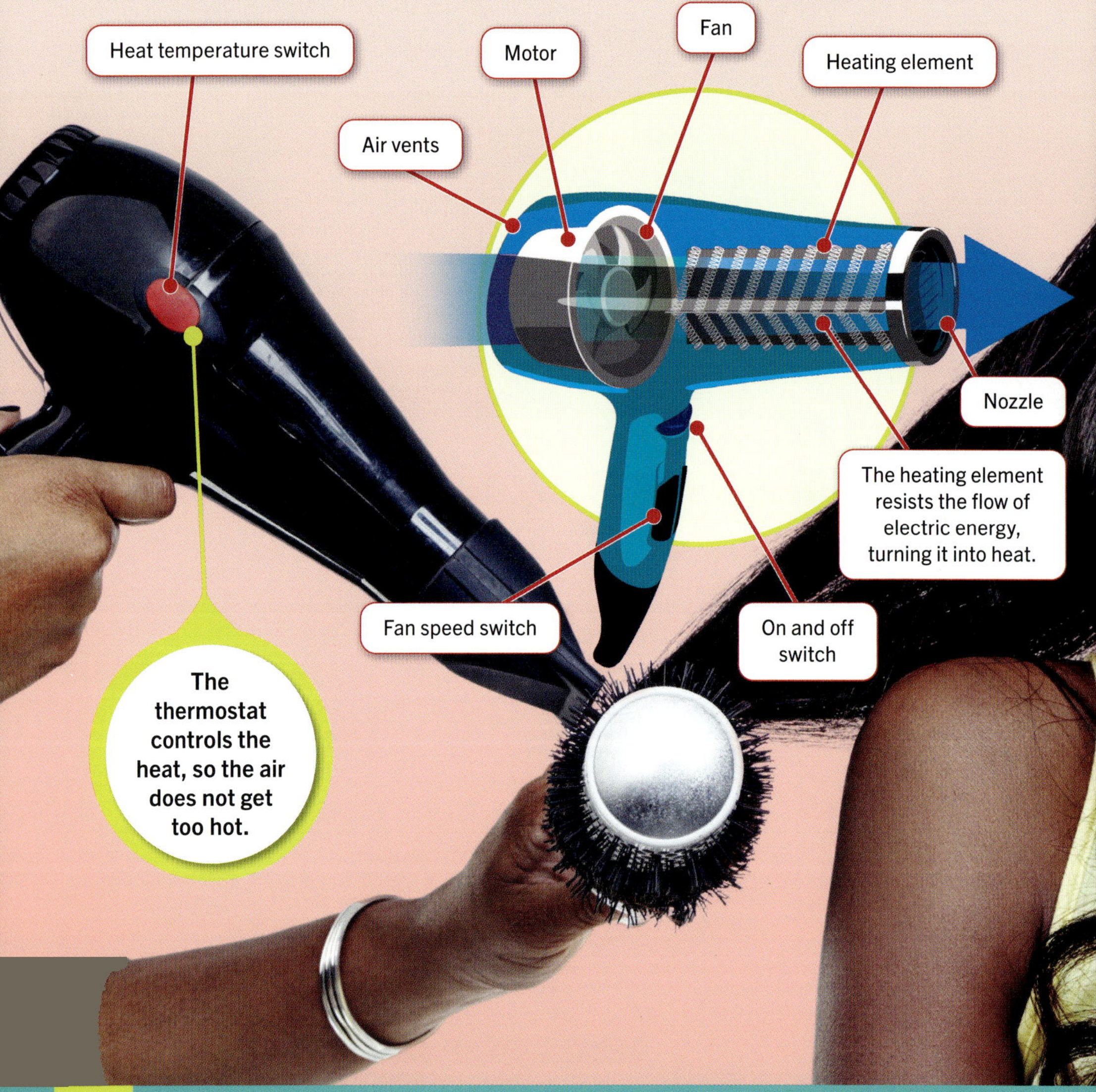

INVENTOR

Inventor: Alexander Godefroy

Invention: Hair dryer

Date: 1890

The story: French hairdresser Alexander Godefroy invented the first hair dryer. His customers sat on a chair and wore a cap that was attached to the chimney pipe of a gas stove to dry their hair with the chimney's heat.

Quiet Hair Dryer

Engineers have produced a lighter, quieter design for a hair dryer. Its intelligent heating control prevents the air from becoming too hot.

Sensors measure exit air temperature 20 times per second. It sends the data to a microprocessor, which monitors the heating element.

Blades spin around up to 110,000 times per minute at an inaudible frequency.

A rubber isolation mount stops the electric motor from vibrating against the casing. This reduces noise.

DID YOU KNOW? The first handheld hair dryer was produced in 1920. It was made of metal and was very heavy.

Smart Homes

Many homes today are fully wired and humming with activity. With an internet connection, most appliances, utilities, and digital devices can be controlled remotely by a cell phone.

Smart appliances allow you to adjust the technology from thousands of miles away.

Smart home appliances and devices can all be hardwired or wirelessly connected together. A person can control their home's heat, air conditioning, door and window locks, security cameras, indoor and outdoor lights, refrigerator, and TV by using their smartphone, tablet, computer, or game console as a remote control.

Smart home appliances can learn your habits and schedules to adjust their operations accordingly. For example, a smart thermostat can learn when you come and go regularly. If you tend to return home every day at 5 p.m., the smart home can change the heat or air conditioning setting to your preferred temperature before you arrive.

DID YOU KNOW? Using motion sensor technology, a smart home can alert both you and the police if intruders enter your empty house.

INVENTOR

Inventor: Nikola Tesla

The invention: Remote control

Date: 1898

The story: Even before radio technology was patented, Nikola Tesla used it to design a radio-controlled steel boat. Radio signals controlled switches that powered the boat's propeller, rudder, and running lights.

Clean Energy for the Future

Technology is always changing and innovating. Just 100 years ago, most homes in North America did not have electricity, running water, or indoor plumbing. The air above our towns and cities was often polluted by coal smoke and gas fumes.

Today, however, we are generating cleaner energy with less pollution using wind, water, solar, and biothermal power. Our homes can be lit, heated, cooled, and powered by this clean energy, and all of their devices, appliances, and utilities can be networked together and remote-controlled by our smartphones.

In the near future, our energy needs may be met by power stations that tap into the extreme heat from volcanoes or fuel cells that are powered by hydrogen harvested from the moon. Our increasingly advanced smart homes may be able to oversee and direct a team of robots that can clean, cook, and do yard work. What kinds of new energy sources and home gadgets can you dream up? With a lot of studying, hard work, and testing, maybe you will make that dream a reality!

Some lights let you change the color or brightness with an app on your phone or smart device.

Review and Reflect

Now that you've read about technology used to harness energy and make homes more livable, let's review what you've learned. Use the following questions to reflect on your newfound knowledge and integrate it with what you already knew.

Check for Understanding

1. How do rechargeable batteries get new power? *(See pp. 6–7)*
2. What is the role of a turbine in hydropower and in wind power? *(See pp. 8–9)*
3. What are the parts of a solar cell? How do they create an electric current? *(See pp. 10–11)*
4. What are the risks of nuclear power? What safety measures are in place to avoid them? *(See pp. 12–13)*
5. Name the three ways energy from organic matter can be captured and used. *(See pp. 14–15)*
6. Describe two ways running water is used in a house and what technology helps make that happen. *(See pp. 18–19)*

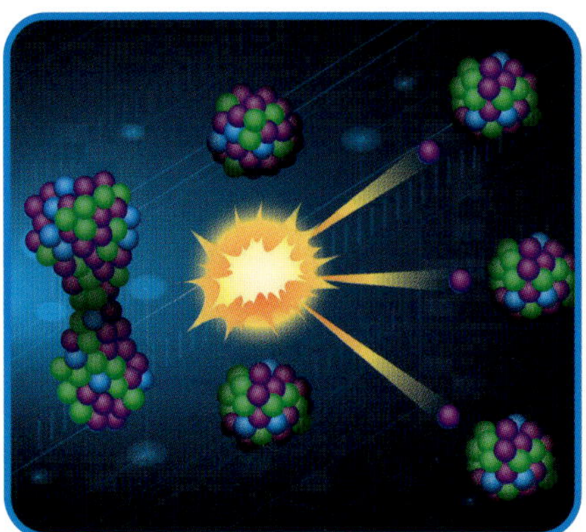

7. Name three parts of a washing machine and explain what each one does. *(See pp. 20–21)*
8. Why do flush toilets use water? What does the water do? *(See pp. 22–23)*
9. Explain how a wastewater treatment plant cleans dirty water. *(See pp. 24–25)*
10. What is gray water? Why would someone want to collect it? *(See pp. 26–27)*
11. How are incandescent light bulbs similar to solid-state lighting? How are they different? *(See pp. 28–29)*
12. How do gas ovens work? How do electric ovens work? How do induction cooktops work? *(See pp. 30–31)*
13. Name three parts of a microwave and explain how each one works. *(See pp. 32–33)*
14. What is the role of gas in how a refrigerator works? *(See pp. 34–35)*
15. Explain how a hair dryer works. *(See pp. 38–39)*

Making Connections

1. Choose two inventors mentioned in the book. What did each one make? How did their inventions affect the way people live?

2. Which devices or tools in this book use batteries? What are the advantages and problems with batteries?

3. Compare and contrast solar power and nuclear power. Where does the energy come from? How is it collected?

4. Think about how running water systems are connected to wastewater treatment plants. How do they work together? Where might they overlap?

5. Choose any two types of technology mentioned in this book to compare and contrast. Describe two similarities and two differences between them.

In Your Own Words

1. Which of the inventions listed in this book do you think is most valuable? Why?

2. What do you think are the benefits of connecting home appliances to the internet? What are some possible drawbacks?

3. Choose one of the tools or devices mentioned in this book that you use regularly. Imagine what your life would be like if it didn't exist. What would be different?

4. Imagine a household technology or tool that you would find useful that doesn't exist yet. What might need to happen before it could be developed?

5. What do you think is the most environmentally important technology mentioned in this book? What makes it so important?

Glossary

aeration the process by which air is circulated through, mixed with, or dissolved in a liquid or substance

biofuel a fuel obtained from living or recently living biological material

capacitor a device used to store an electric charge

conductor a material that enables the flow of heat or electricity

electrode a conductor through which electricity enters or leaves an object

electron a particle within an atom that carries a negative charge

filament a piece of thin, coiled wire

induction the production of an electric current made by being close to, but not touching, an electrified or magnetized body

infrared having a wavelength greater than that of the red end of the visible light spectrum but less than that of microwaves

magnetic field a region around a magnet within which the force of magnetism acts

microwaves energy with wavelengths shorter than those of radio waves but longer than those of infrared radiation

photon a particle representing a discrete quantity of light

radiation the emission of energy in the form of electromagnetic waves

radioactive emitting radiation in the form of ionized particles

rudder a flat piece hinged vertically near the stern of a boat for steering

semiconductor a substance, such as silicon, that displays variable resistance to an electrical current

terminal a point of connection for closing an electric circuit

turbine a rotor that is turned by the flow of wind, steam, water, or some other fluid in order to generate power

ultraviolet having a wavelength shorter than that of the violet end of visible light but longer than that of X-rays

vacuum a space from which the air has been removed

valve a device for controlling the passage of fluid through a pipe or duct

voltage a measure of the force of an electrical charge as it moves in a wire or other electrical conductor

Read More

Gitlin, Marty. *The Birth of Modern Tech (American Eras: Defining Moments).* Ann Arbor, MI: Cherry Lake Publishing, 2022.

MacCarald, Clara. *All about Green Tech (Cutting-Edge Technology).* Lake Elmo, MN: Focus Readers, 2023.

Nardo, Don. *Tech Innovations Inspired by Nature.* San Diego, CA: ReferencePoint Press, Inc., 2024.

Shea, Therese. *Technologies That Help the Planet (Spotlight on Global Issues).* New York: Rosen Publishing, 2022.

Learn More Online

1. Go to **www.factsurfer.com** or scan the QR code below.
2. Enter "**Energy Home Tech**" into the search box.
3. Click on the cover of this book to see a list of websites.

Index